Living our beliefs

An exploration of the faith and practice of Quakers

Compiled and edited by Graham Ralph with young Quakers

First published February 2016

Quaker Books, Friends House, 173 Euston Road,
London NW1 2BJ

www.quaker.org.uk

ISBN: 978 1 907123 91 7

eISBN: 978 1 907123 92 4

Book designed and typeset by Cox Design: www.coxdesign.co.uk

Illustrations by Rob Pepper

Printed by CM Print, Brighton

Go to www.yqspace.org.uk/living-our-beliefs for online content.

Living our beliefs

*Be patterns, be examples in all countries, places,
islands, nations, wherever you come, that your carriage
and life may preach among all sorts of people, and
to them: then you will come to walk cheerfully over
the world, answering that of God in every one.*
George Fox, 1656

~

Let your life speak.
Advices & queries 27

Acknowledgements

This book has been compiled and edited by Graham Ralph in partnership with young Quakers. In addition to the young people making up the editorial group, a great deal of help has come from various gatherings in 2015: the Young People's Participation Day alongside Meeting for Sufferings (also in 2014), Junior Yearly Meeting, the Young People's Programme and the regional summer events. Quakers in Britain staff, particularly Quaker Life's Children & Young People's Work team, have been an invaluable help and support.

Contents

Additional content can be found online at
www.yqspace.org.uk/living-our-beliefs

Introduction

Young Quakers have for many years wanted a book that
would tackle similar topics to *Quaker faith & practice* but
would be shorter, more accessible and more concise. This
book, *Living our beliefs*, is the response. Living our beliefs is
also available as an ebook at www.yqspace.org.uk/living-
our-beliefs.

Living our beliefs recognises that words have limitations, but
they can still be valuable tools for describing our faith and
journeys. Part of the introduction to *Quaker faith & practice*
expands on this idea: "Words must not become barriers
between us, for no one of us can ever adequately understand
or express the truth about God. Yet words are our tools and
we must not be afraid to express the truth we know in the
best words we can." It is this conviction that has prompted
the selection of a wide variety of extracts for inclusion in
this book, confirming our testimony that truth cannot be
confined within a creed. "We must trust that faith is robust,
compassionate and 'not quick to take offence', and that
the Spirit which gives the words is communicated through
them" (Introduction to *Quaker faith & practice*).

We hope that the words in this book will be tools for
questioning and understanding.

Most chapters in *Living our beliefs* begin with a list of words
relating to the chapter topic. These words start the process
of questioning and discussion. A purposefully brief written
section follows, adding information. The final section of
each chapter consists of quotations selected from a wide
variety of Quaker and other sources, reflecting the belief
that truth can come from many different directions. The

quotations include contemporary and current thoughts that are likely to remain relevant to a wide readership. The editorial team has aimed to include material from younger Quakers, particularly from Junior Yearly Meeting, the Young People's Programme and the regional summer events, in the hope that this will add to the depth and relevance of the book.

Many chapters of *Living our beliefs* include links to web-based material (music and video) that was created at Junior Yearly Meeting 2015 and Britain Yearly Meeting's Young People's Programme 2015.

For the music, young Quakers chose some music tracks that reflected their understandings, experiences or feelings about their Quakerism. Using these suggestions, the young people on the editorial board of *Living our beliefs* created a playlist of the most popular songs as well as playlists for some of the book's chapters. See www.yqspace.org.uk/playlists.

For the video clips, young Quakers explored their thoughts and feelings on which passage of *Quaker faith & practice* was their favourite. Participants were recorded reading their favourite passage and in some cases sharing why the passage they had read was important to them. The young people's editorial board for *Living our beliefs* agreed the video clips to be used and the chapter of the book that each related to. See www.yqspace.org.uk/passages.

Although the motivation for *Living our beliefs* came from young Quakers, the potential use and readership of the book are much wider. Those new to Quakers and those who want a concise, informative introduction should also find it helpful. Because of this, we have used the name 'Quaker', which many people are familiar with, rather than 'Friend' (the name Quakers use to each other). The word 'Friend' has been used where it is a part of a quotation or is correct usage, for example in the title 'Religious Society of Friends'.

Living our beliefs is not a definitive document; the compiler and editorial board hope that it will be revised over time as people in our Quaker communities reflect on their lives and beliefs. "Only what we have valued and truly made our own, not by assertion but by lives of faithful commitment, can we hand on to the future. Even then, our vision of the truth will again and again be amended" (Introduction to *Quaker faith & practice*).

Who are Quakers?

Equality | Friends of truth

Integrity | 'Let your life speak'

Peace | Simplicity

Testimonies | Witness

The Religious Society of Friends, more commonly known as Quakers, is guided by the understanding that there is 'that of God' in everyone. While recognising that 'God' means different things to different people, Quakers hold that every person is able to come to know God's love directly, without priests or rituals. Quakers believe in the importance of a continuing search by each individual for increasing knowledge and understanding. It is from this that the values of speaking truth, treating human beings with respect, living simply, striving for community, and resolving conflict through peaceful means can naturally unfold.

Quakers follow a way of life rather than a list of rules. Conviction is gained by looking at our innermost hearts. This experience cannot ultimately be described in words, but Quakers base their whole lives on it.

The Quaker movement sprang from the teachings of a group of men and a few women, led by George Fox, who found that established religion provided insufficient guidance and comfort. Fox walked over northern England in the mid 1600s seeking spiritual direction. The followers of the movement called themselves the 'Friends of Truth'. They believed that their experience of a direct, unmediated communion with God was available to all people everywhere.

A hundred years later, the American Quaker John Woolman expressed this belief in these words: 'There is a principle which... in different places and ages hath different names; it is, however, pure and proceeds from God. It is deep and inward, confined to no forms of religion nor excluded from anywhere the heart stands in perfect sincerity. In whomsoever this takes root and grows, of what nation soever, they become brethren' (John Woolman, 1762; *Quaker faith & practice* 26.61).

These values and understandings have led Quakers to convictions about how we may follow our beliefs in our lives. Each one of us has a responsibility to discover, in ourselves and in others, that light and truth that is unique.

This responsibility is woven into the everyday through the testimonies that help us reflect on what we do in our lives: testimonies to peace and conflict, truth and integrity, equality, simplicity, service, stewardship and sustainability. These testimonies are not rules but what Quakers traditionally call 'understandings' that have developed from the lived experience of putting our faith into action. The testimonies reflect the society we interact with and so have changed over time. They help us examine our relationship with others in our communities, the environment, the society and the world we live in. The testimonies arise out of a deep, inner conviction, may challenge our normal ways of living, and may mean taking a stand against common social practices. We become who we are by what we do.

For online content go to
www.yqspace.org.uk/passages
www.yqspace.org.uk/playlists

⌀

Let your life speak.
Advices & queries 27

⌀

Take time to learn about other people's experiences of the Light.
While respecting the experiences of others, do not be afraid
to say what you have found and what you value. Appreciate
that doubt and questioning can also lead to spiritual growth
and to a greater awareness of the Light that is in us all.
Advices & queries 5

⌀

I am a Quaker. I am part of a worldwide Quaker community
and I inhabit that knowledge daily. It helps me live the way
I want to. The knowledge and reality of that community
membership informs my life and gives me the strength I need to
live faithfully, to speak truth to power, to witness in the world.
Ben Pink Dandelion, *Celebrating the Quaker Way*

⌀

The circumstances of modern life give far too little
nourishment to our common humanity – to goodness,
courage, common sense, reflection, wonder, patience,
understanding – to what the Greek philosopher Plato
called "our mysterious preference for the best".
Robert Lawrence Smith, *A Quaker book of wisdom*

⌀

~

*Through the examples of current and past Quakers we are
helped to explore and question our way of life within the
Religious Society of Friends and our wider community.*
Participant, Northern Young Friends Summer Shindig 2015

~

Think it possible that you may be mistaken.
Advices & queries 17

~

*Quakers do not deny human weakness, but their tendency is
instead to give thanks for human strength. They believe in
the essential goodness of people, so they deny the notion that
we are by nature 'miserable sinners' and reject the habits and
customs that go with it... They do not want religious ritual,
symbol or costume to get in the way of their unmediated
communion with the divine. It is in that relationship that
they find their energy and spirit. They are not so much
staring into the darkness, as standing in the Light.*
Geoffrey Durham, *Being a Quaker.*

~

*Don't be ashamed of your religion; stand up for what
you believe in; don't be a victim of authority.*
Participant, Yorkshire Friends Holiday School 2015

~

~

I am a Quaker, completely, I don't think of it as a belief, it is just the way that I am... it's my identity, it is not about deciding you're a Quaker, it is about realising you're a Quaker... We are not Quakers because we are good, but because we are not.
Ben Pink Dandelion, *Celebrating the Quaker Way*

~

No one person can fully understand God or express His words or wishes fully. No matter how well intended rules are, if they are followed mindlessly they will lose their meaning and we will lose our touch with God and what God truly wants. Only through discussion and stillness can we try to learn.
Participant, Northern Young Friends Summer Shindig 2015

~

Meeting for worship

Gathered | *Listening*

Ministry | *Reflection*

Sharing | *Silence*

As a community, Quakers gather quietly for meeting for worship on most Sunday mornings. Meeting for worship starts as soon as the first person enters the room. Quakers will gather in silence; meeting is a silent waiting, listening for God's truth. At its best the silence is not just an absence of noise; it is a seeking for quietness of mind, of body and of spirit. In meeting we try to find the presence of God inside ourselves by listening and waiting. This is a shared occasion where the people in meeting all have the same aim; it is this sharing that makes the meeting a collective experience. The children of the meeting will likely have their own gathering but will probably join the main meeting for the first or last 15 minutes. The end of meeting for worship is indicated when two Quakers shake hands.

Meeting for worship can be entirely silent, but often someone will stand and speak. This 'ministry' will reflect their own personal search for the truth inside themselves. Any person may be moved to stand and speak during meeting, and people will be happy to hear ideas and truths presented by a variety of people in many different ways. We are asked to listen quietly and respectfully and with open minds – we don't have to be of the same mind; we are all free to discern our own understanding of the Light. Spoken ministry may spring from many different sources. Each of us brings our own experiences, and Quakers will look for the underlying truth in what is spoken.

In the quietness of a Quaker meeting we may become aware of a powerful spirit of love and truth; we may feel that we have shared that of God that exists within each of us. Meeting for worship can be held anywhere or at any time. Many of us have experienced meeting on a hill, in a hotel lobby or under the stars; it is often on these occasions, with others, that the silence can surprise and the spirit can burn even more brightly.

~

*We listened and heard the silence. We listened and felt
the silence. We listened and tasted the silence. We closed
our eyes and saw the great silence dwelling within.*
Moses Shongo, a Seneca elder, 1800s

~

*Lying upon a mound of rocks in a field somewhere near
Yealand. Looking at the sky in total silence created an
atmosphere of stillness and peace. It was the only meeting I
have ever done outside and this made the silence seem so much
more pure. The meeting halls of Bootham and Brigflatts may
be beautiful but they were beaten by the beauty of having
nothing. The darkness cast a spell over the meeting and
closed the world in, making our togetherness feel absolute.*
Felix Charteris, student, Bootham School, York

~

*True worship may be experienced at any time, in any place –
alone on the hills or in the busy daily life – we may find God...
But this individual experience is not sufficient, and in a meeting
held in the Spirit there is a giving and receiving between its
members, one helping another with or without words.*
Quaker faith & practice 2.11

~

~

*For me the focused, expectant silence of the meeting was like
nothing I'd ever experienced. Birdsong or traffic noises would
mingle with the occasional cough, or creak of a seat, within the
room. And after perhaps ten minutes there would be a sense of
the silence deepening – like a coastal shelf falling away beneath
our feet. A profound, inner stillness would descend as fidgeting
diminished and superficial sounds receded into the background.*
Tom Robinson (b. 1950)

~

*We need to find God, and he cannot be found in noise
and restlessness. God is the friend of silence. See how
nature – trees, flowers, grass – grows in silence; see
the stars, the moon and the sun, how they move in
silence... We need silence to be able to touch souls.*
Mother Teresa (1910–1997)

~

*The beauty of silence is that it allows us to engage where
we are. We are not dovetailed into someone else's sermon,
neither are our devotions determined by an outward
liturgy. Rather, our motions of faith can sit where they
need to be, close to us in their authenticity and sincerity,
closer to God in their directness and individuality.*
Ben Pink Dandelion, *Celebrating the Quaker Way*

~

~

*In silence we can discover the divine within, which is universally
accessible but speaks to each of us in a unique voice. If we
can locate, at the very centre of silence, our individual 'still
small voice', we will have found our greatest ally in life.
Because if we listen to that voice with an open heart, it will
guide us through the most challenging crossroads of our
lives: in work, in love, in distinguishing right from wrong.*
Robert Lawrence Smith, *A Quaker book of wisdom*

~

*Silence gives everyone the chance to be heard, which in
turn creates equality. In our busy world it is incredibly
important to stop and appreciate silence every once
in a while. Too much noise can be suffocating.*
Participant, Yorkshire Friends Holiday School 2015

~

Be still and know that I am God.
Psalms 46:10

~

*Don't feel restricted by the silence, it is there to set you free from
the pressures of life. No-one is judging your movements, your
thoughts... Freedom of expression is the freedom to worship God
on your own terms. Value the opportunity to think unguided
by the world. Learn what you feel you need to know, let other
information pass. No moment of silence is a waste of time.*
Rachel Needham, 1987; *Quaker faith & practice* 2.17

~

*Silence can be more than just nothing. It can
invade our senses and provoke our thoughts.*
Participant, Britain Yearly Meeting Young People's
Programme 2015

~

*Silence is more than just a lack of noise, but
is a feeling inside, 'dwelling within'.*
Participant, Yorkshire Friends Holiday School, 2015

~

*It's easy to be alone and think for yourself and gather your
own thoughts in silence, but it's even more powerful to be
together in the silence and to feel linked with others.*
Participant, Junior Yearly Meeting 2015

~

Are you open to new light, from whatever source it may come?
Advices & queries 7

~

Belief in action

Discernment | Respect

Responsibility | Service

Sharing | Witness

Quakers believe that there is that of God in every one. Thus we try to respond to need wherever it exists, in whomever it exists, not just among our friends but wherever we can. Working for others as service, the act of helping someone, is love made visible and helps both the giver and the receiver.

It is possible that some of us may have a blinding flash or revelation about what we are called to do. However, it is more likely that this awareness will arrive after a time of reflection, consideration, gathering information and comparing opinions, testing out in our mind and in our heart how we feel. The decision to take action can be quite simple and intuitive; in other situations the decision may be more complex and involved. It is likely that meeting for worship and our interactions with other Quakers will play a significant part in this process of discernment.

We are all moved to serve in different ways. Quakers have worked for the abolition of slavery, for prison reform, for the Friends Ambulance Unit, as hospice volunteers, for asylum seekers and refugees, for homeless people and in soup kitchens. Quakers have taken part in demonstrations, become politically involved, volunteered for work abroad, 'spoken truth to power' by writing letters privately and/or publicly. It may be right to be involved with the workings of your local meeting or with Quaker groups; and it is always possible that you will be called on to listen to a friend, to be with someone, to hold someone in the Light, to hold their hand, to give them a hug or just bake them a cake!

Our faith and our witness in the world are inseparable – each feeds the other. The Quaker testimonies to peace, integrity, equality and simplicity provide signposts to what we are led to do. Our actions can make the world a better place.

For online content go to
www.yqspace.org.uk/passages
www.yqspace.org.uk/playlists
www.yqspace.org.uk/bethechange

~

I expect to pass through this world but once. Any good
therefore that I can do, or any kindness that I can show
to any fellow creature, let me do it now. Let me not defer
or neglect it, for I shall not pass this way again.
Stephen Grellet (1773–1855)

~

Respect the laws of the state and consider your moral purposes.
If you have a strong conviction to break the law, search your
conscience deeply and seek the advice of others you trust.
Participant, Northern Young Friends Summer Shindig 2015

~

O brother man! Fold to thy heart thy brother;
Where pity dwells, the peace of God is there;
To worship rightly is to love each other,
Each smile a hymn, each kindly deed a prayer.
John Greenleaf Whittier (1807–1892)

~

Love your neighbour as you love yourself.
Matthew 19:19

~

~

*Live adventurously. When choices arise, do you take
the way that offers the fullest opportunity for the use of
your gifts in the service of God and the community?*
Advices & queries 27

~

*I believe that we are most ourselves when we are
connecting with others through service.*
Robert Lawrence Smith, *A Quaker book of wisdom*

~

*Let me light my lamp, says the star, and never
debate if it will help remove the darkness.*
Rabindranath Tagore (1861–1941)

~

Be the change you want to see in the world.
Mahatma Gandhi (1869–1948)

~

*You can change and inspire by saying what needs to
be said. You have more power than you know.*
Participant, Friends Summer School 2015

~

~

Past the seeker as he prayed came the cripple and the beggar and the beaten. And seeing them the Holy One went down into deep prayer and cried, "Great God, how is it that a loving creator can see such things and yet do nothing about them?" And out of the long silence, God said, "I did do something. I made you."
Sufi teaching

~

A young girl was walking along a beach where thousands of starfish had been washed up during a storm. When she came to each starfish, she would pick it up and throw it back into the ocean. She had been doing this for some time when a man approached her and said, "Why are you doing this? Look at all the starfish on the beach! You can't begin to make a difference!" The girl listened, paused and after a few moments bent down, picked up another starfish and hurled it as far as she could into the ocean, saying: "I made a difference to that one!"
Adapted from Loren C. Eiseley (1907–1977)

~

The Light is available yesterday, today and to eternity. What is thee doing about it?
Lucretia Mott (1793–1880)

~

There is hope. Lots of hope.
Participant, Britain Yearly Meeting Young People's Programme 2015

~

Truth and integrity

Honesty | *Integrity*

Respect | *Sincerity*

Trust | *Truth*

Quakers use 'Truth' to mean the universal values, principles and convictions of the life led by the spirit inside us. The concept is also seen as demanding honest, simple speech and a refusal to countenance the double standards of saying one thing and doing another. Truth is an integral part of the Quaker testimony to the Light within us all. We can only be true to our innermost self if we are faithful to the truth and honest in our dealings. Truth and integrity are fundamental guiding principles in our own lives and also in our community engagement. Early Quaker artisans and shopkeepers soon acquired a reputation for honesty and fair prices. Their integrity was a key factor in their great success in business and banking in the 18th and 19th centuries.

Quakers believe it is important to tell others about the truth as we see it. 'Speaking truth to power' means telling people with influence about your concerns and standing up for what you see is right when you think something is wrong.

The testimony to truth and integrity is essentially a call for consistency between what you think and say about yourself and what you actually do. To be the best you can, what you think needs to come out in what you say and do. Quakers have always refused to swear oaths (in court or anywhere else), because promising "to tell the truth, the whole truth, and nothing but the truth" in court would imply that they did not promise to tell the truth everywhere else.

And how do we know what the truth is? When Quakers attend meeting for worship and listen to ministry, they may be searching for the truth. When we read and respond to *Advices and queries*, we are searching for the truth. This search will never end and we are likely to challenge ourselves time and again at different stages of our lives and in different circumstances. Answering honestly and with integrity is not a small matter. Then, when we have answered honestly, we can decide what to do, never forgetting that 'we are what we do'.

For online content go to
www.yqspace.org.uk/playlists

~

*Dearly beloved Friends, these things we do not lay upon you as
a rule or form to walk by; but that all, with a measure of the
light, which is pure and holy, may be guided: and so in the light
walking and abiding, these things may be fulfilled in the Spirit,
not in the letter, for the letter killeth, but the Spirit giveth life.*
Postscript to an epistle from the elders in Balby, 1656;
Introduction to *Advices & queries*

~

*Take heed, dear Friends, to the promptings of love and
truth in your hearts. Trust them as the leadings of God,
whose light shows us our darkness and brings us new life.*
Advices & queries 1

~

*Three things cannot hide for long: the
Moon, the Sun and the Truth.*
Gautama Buddha

~

*Integrity is a bugger, it really is. Lying can get
you into difficulties, but to really wind up in the
crappers try telling nothing but the truth.*
David Mitchell, *Ghostwritten*

~

~

*Live your truth. Express your love. Share your
enthusiasm. Take action towards your dreams. Walk
your talk. Dance and sing to your music. Embrace
your blessings. Make today worth remembering.*
Steve Maraboli

~

*Truth is like the sun. You can shut it out
for a time, but it ain't going away.*
Elvis Presley (1935–1977)

~

*Live adventurously. When choices arise, do you take the way
that offers the fullest opportunity for the use of your gifts in
the service of God and the community? Let your life speak.*
Advices & queries 27

~

*This above all,
To thine own self be true,
And it must follow as the night the day,
Thou canst not then be false to any man.*
William Shakespeare, *Hamlet*

~

*Truth resides in every human heart, and one has to search for it
there, and to be guided by truth as one sees it. But no one has a
right to coerce others to act according to his own view of truth.*
Mahatma Gandhi (1869–1948)

~

~

If pressure is brought upon you to lower your standard of integrity, are you prepared to resist it? Our responsibilities to God and our neighbour may involve us taking unpopular stands. Do not let the desire to be sociable, or the fear of being peculiar, determine your decision.
Advices & queries 38

~

Everyone's truth is different. It's how you use the truth which counts.
Participant, Friends Summer School 2015

~

Peace and conflict

Conflict resolution | Empathy

Nonviolence | Pacifism

Reconciliation | Seeds of war

Trust | Understanding

William Penn said, "We are too ready to retaliate, rather than forgive, or gain by love and information. And yet we could hurt no man that we believe loves us. Let us then try what Love will do: for if men did once see we love them, we should soon find they would not harm us" (William Penn, 1693; *Quaker faith & practice* 23:03). The act of love is at the centre of the Quaker peace testimony. We are asked to try what love will do in all parts of our lives and the world, not just by working on a national or global scale but by looking at our relationships and activities at all levels.

As Quakers we believe that our faith should be lived out practically in our actions. Working for peace can be a consequence of this wanting to live our beliefs. Handling conflict creatively can be a force for positive change and is more than just winning and losing. Many Quakers are pacifists as a matter of conscience, because we are asked to look for the love and truth in the hearts of others and ourselves. Violent actions contradict the search for the God in our lives.

The testimony to peace calls on us to strive for harmony among all people, nations and individuals. If we recognise that we all have a spark of God within, we try not to harm one another or to treat others aggressively. If we treat all people as if they have the same spirit within them that we have in ourselves, we practise equality. If we seek to eliminate conditions of inequality in the world, and to value people above possessions, we encourage simplicity.

From their beginning, Quakers have been known for taking a stand for peace and against military action. "During the world wars, Quakers took different paths. Some felt they had to join the armed forces, but many decided they could not" (Isabel Cartwright, 2014). Working for this kind of peace can be difficult. Those who served in the Friends Ambulance Unit (founded by Quakers in World War I) were brave indeed, as were those who were imprisoned in the world wars because they would not compromise on their beliefs and would not join up. Some Quakers may choose to join peaceful demonstrations, to work with the Alternatives to Violence Project, to take relief into areas recently ravaged by war or to give funds for peace education. Our inner voice will help tell us what course of action we are to pursue. We respond individually to what the spirit requires of us.

As Quakers we also try to live out our commitment to peace in every part of our lives. We may set up and support long-term individual and collective Quaker action as an expression of our peace testimony. We may develop and support alternative ways of resolving and engaging with conflicts, working for a reduction in armaments and a change to the conditions and circumstances that lead to war. Tackling the seeds of war is central to our testimony to peace. Simply 'bearing witness' to a different way – a way that affirms the value of all life rather than denies it through violence – is something we can all do. This too is an important part of our peace testimony. We all have a role to play with our neighbours, in our school or college, among our friends and wider community, in our family, in our workplace and with our colleagues and peers. We each do what we can.

Conflict is inevitable at times in most human relationships and we can learn from interaction with those who disagree with our own view of the world. Empathetic understanding of another's viewpoint is vital when seeking to undo some of the hurt in the world and to build a better future. To be nonviolent is an active process in all our lives. As Penn said, "Let us then try what Love will do."

For online content go to
www.yqspace.org.uk/passages
www.yqspace.org.uk/playlists
www.yqspace.org.uk/bethechange

~

The peace testimony is about deeds not creeds;
not a form of words but a way of living.
Quaker faith & practice 24.11

~

You can choose whether you love and forgive or
stay angry forever. Choose forgiveness.
Participant, Friends Summer School 2015

~

Each time a person stands up for an ideal, or acts to
improve the lot of others, or strikes out against injustice,
he or she sends forth a ripple of hope. Crossing each
other from a million different centres of energy and
daring, those ripples build a current that can sweep down
the mightiest walls of oppression and resistance.
Robert F. Kennedy (1925–1968)

~

A grandfather was talking to his grandson about how he
felt about a tragedy. He said, "I feel as if I have two wolves
fighting in my heart. One wolf is the vengeful, angry, violent
one. The other wolf is the loving, compassionate one." The
grandson asked him, "Which wolf will win the fight in your
heart?" The grandfather answered, "The one I feed."
A Cherokee legend

~

~

*Conflict happens, and will continue to happen, even
in the most peaceful of worlds. And that's good – a
world where we all agreed with one another would be
incredibly boring. Our differences help us to learn.*
Quaker faith & practice 20.71

~

*A good end cannot sanctify evil means; nor must
we ever do evil, that good may come of it.*
William Penn, 1693; Quaker faith & practice 24.03

~

*Peace is a journey and a way of life rather than something in
the distance – it is more achievable than some think it is.*
Participant, Junior Yearly Meeting 2015

~

*Peace is not a distant goal that we seek, but the
means by which we arrive at that goal.*
Martin Luther King, Jr. (1929–1968)

~

*The places to begin acquiring the skills and maturity and
generosity to avoid or to resolve conflicts are in our own homes,
our personal relationships, our schools, our workplaces.*
Yearly Meeting of Aotearoa/New Zealand, 1987

~

~

*All bloody principles and practices we do utterly deny,
with all outward wars, and strife, and fightings with
outward weapons, for any end, or under any pretence
whatsoever, and this is our testimony to the whole world.*
Quaker Declaration to Charles II, 1660

~

*Nonviolence is by no means a passive or negative
concept, a simple thou-shalt-not-kill prohibition. It is a
springboard for action, an ideal that must be transformed
into the active pursuit of peace and justice.*
Robert Lawrence Smith, *A Quaker book of wisdom*

~

*If we are angry we know how wars develop. It
does not matter who's wrong. What matters is
that we care enough to talk to each other.*
Quaker faith & practice 20.68

~

*The past two years have been some of the richest and most
transformative of my life. So often I have found myself wanting
to package and contain a moment, an interaction or an
experience, to somehow breathe it in and make it a permanent
part of my own organism... I have felt it when listening to Pastor
Sebastian who forgave the man who plotted to kill him during
the war... His story has sunk into my heart and has grown in
me a desire to continue coming alongside these kinds of effort.*
Elin Henrysson, Quaker peaceworker in Burundi 2010–2012

~

Equality

Diversity | Fairness

Justice | Love

Respect | Understanding

Quakers recognise the equal worth and unique nature of every person. The belief in equality, sharing and community will often conflict with a world where self-importance and materialism can appear so central. If we stop supporting each other we risk despair, alienation and rejection, especially for those who find society a difficult place to be.

Early Quakers supported the equal spiritual authority of women and refused to use words, titles or actions that recognised or reinforced social inequalities. Using 'thee' or 'thou' and refusing to take off your hat may belong to the past, but today we address people by their first and second names only, rejecting titles (even the ordinary ones such as 'Mr', 'Mrs', 'Miss' or 'Ms'). Some Quakers may refuse to accept 'honours' of the kind given by the Queen, or, if they do accept them, certainly wouldn't use their titles in a Quaker setting.

Our concern for equality also involves looking at the way in which our own lifestyle and behaviour can potentially increase inequalities. We may be aware of issues concerning social inclusion, ethical investment, fair trade, the avoidance of exploitation and discrimination, work with the homeless, asylum seekers, refugees and prisoners, and prison reform. Our concern for equality is a testimony of increasing relevance in today's complex and multicultural society, in which there is an acute need for racial justice and for empathy between all faiths.

In recent years our testimony to equality has led us as Quakers to change our marriage procedures. Before official new regulations were introduced (December 2011) in England, Wales and Scotland, Britain Yearly Meeting decided to seek to change the law to allow same-sex marriage in the same way as opposite-sex marriage in Quaker meetings. Quakers are clear that "the right joining in marriage is the work of the Lord only, and not the priests' or magistrates'" (George Fox, 1669).

The belief that there is that of God in everyone constantly challenges us in terms of equality. The questions that emerge from this belief are inescapable. We are led to go into our homes, workplaces, schools, shops, council chambers, country and world and seek equality for everyone. We are what we do.

For online content go to
www.yqspace.org.uk/playlists

~

*Quakers' commitment to equality is an essential
component of all their testimonies. You can't have
truth, simplicity or peace without it. And, as with those
testimonies, this one to equality is infused with love.*
Geoffrey Durham, *Being a Quaker*

~

*I have a dream that my four little children will one day
live in a nation where they will not be judged by the color
of their skin, but by the content of their character.*
Martin Luther King, Jr. (1929–1968)

~

*Refrain from making prejudiced judgements
about the life journeys of others.*
Advices & queries 22

~

*Do you respect that of God in everyone though it
may be expressed in unfamiliar ways or be difficult
to discern?... Listen patiently and seek the truth that
other people's opinions may contain for you.*
Advices & queries 17

~

*If we cannot now end our differences, at least we
can help make the world safe for diversity.*
John F. Kennedy (1917–1963)

~

~

Gender equality is more than a goal in itself. It is a precondition for meeting the challenge of reducing poverty, promoting sustainable development and building good governance.
Kofi Annan (b. 1938)

~

Are you working to bring about a just and compassionate society which allows everyone to develop their capacities and fosters the desire to serve?
Advices & queries 33

~

As you grow up, always tell the truth, do no harm to others, and don't think you are the most important being on earth. Rich or poor, you then can look anyone in the eye and say, "I'm probably no better than you, but I'm certainly your equal."
Harper Lee (b. 1926), letter

~

Are you alert to practices here and throughout the world which discriminate against people on the basis of who or what they are or because of their beliefs? Bear witness to the humanity of all people, including those who break society's conventions or its laws.
Advices & queries 33

~

~

Am I respectful of all persons regardless of race,
ethnicity, religion, culture, gender, income, age, sexual
orientation, physical or learning differences?
Faith and Practice, Friends School of Baltimore

~

There's a light that is shining in the heart of a man
It's the light that was shining when the world began.
There's a light that is shining in the Turk and the Jew
And a light that is shining, friend, in me and in you.
Sydney Carter (1915–2004)

~

We discovered that it is acceptable to have confused feelings, to
be different, to do things our own way. We should not feel guilty
when we are wrong, and appreciate that there must be room for
mistakes. There are people who want us to be exactly as we are.
Epistle of Junior Yearly Meeting 1991;
Quaker faith & practice 21.06

~

Simplicity

Appreciation | *Balance*

Clearness | *Priority*

Reality | *Truth*

M any people are concerned about the excesses and unfairness of the 'consumer society' and the unsustainable use of our world's natural resources. Many try to live simply and to allow space for those things in our lives that really matter: the people around us, the environment and our spiritual experiences. Quakers believe that it is hard to concentrate on what really matters if our lives are dominated by worldly distractions: acquiring wealth and possessions, gambling, spending on alcohol and drugs, worrying too much about fashion and appearances, or taking too much pride in accomplishments.

Seeking simplicity involves trying to allow the divine to infuse our lives. This may lead us to question the way we live and recognise what our true needs are. We should be aware of how our own standard of living is sometimes achieved at the expense of others. Many of us are part of a privileged group of people, and we have a great deal to give to each other and to the world around us.

The Quaker form of worship reflects our striving for simplicity. We do not have clergy, icons or idols, a set creed or prayers, or altars or hymns. Robert L. Smith said: "All you need for worship is a quiet place out-of-doors or a plain meeting house. All you need to share the light within and help find truth is plain, clear language among seekers. All you need for living are a few possessions, simplicity of spirit, and readiness to answer to the divine spark in every person" (Robert Lawrence Smith, *A Quaker book of wisdom*). Meeting for worship also allows us time away from the busyness of a crowded world.

Living simply and finding opportunities to devote our time and resources to what really matters doesn't mean we live boring, unexciting lives. We are advised to 'live adventurously', to search for the ways we might make a difference to ourselves and others. If we find ways to be fulfilled, we can be much more effective for others and the world around us. The testimony to simplicity can be exciting and challenging. Sharing time with our friends and relatives and colleagues, informing ourselves, and finding out what we should be doing next... all these are part of our testimony to simplicity. Finding out who we are and who we might grow to be, can enable us to discern what we don't want and what we don't need. In this way we can discover what really matters.

For online content go to
www.yqspace.org.uk/passages
www.yqspace.org.uk/playlists

~

*Unnecessary possessions are unnecessary burdens. If
you have them, you have to take care of them! There
is great freedom in simplicity of living. It is those who
have enough but not too much who are the happiest.*
Peace Pilgrim

~

*Drop thy still dews of quietness,
Till all our strivings cease;
Take from our souls the strain and stress,
And let our ordered lives confess
The beauty of thy peace.*
John Greenleaf Whittier (1807–1892)

~

*Simplicity is not just simple clothes and a simple lifestyle.
It's an organization of the mind that enables you to sort out
the unimportant details that often clutter your thoughts.*
Student, Sidwell School, Washington, DC

~

*In order to improve your life, you need to appreciate
what you have already. Simple everyday things such as
playing in the garden as a child are very special to me,
even though they seemed ordinary at the time. I guess
that causes me to reconsider my priorities sometimes.*
Participant, Friends Southern Senior Conference 2015

~

~

A common man marvels at uncommon things.
A wise man marvels at the commonplace.
Confucius (551–479BC)

~

'Tis the gift to be simple, 'tis the gift to be free
'Tis the gift to come down where we ought to be,
And when we find ourselves in the place just right,
'Twill be in the valley of love and delight.
When true simplicity is gained,
To bow and to bend we shan't be ashamed,
To turn, turn will be our delight,
Till by turning, turning we come 'round right.
Joseph Brackett, Shaker elder, 1848

~

Try to live simply. A simple lifestyle freely chosen is a
source of strength. Do not be persuaded into buying
what you do not need or cannot afford. Do you keep
yourself informed about the effects your style of living
is having on the global economy and environment?
Advices & queries 41

~

~

*I ask for daily bread, but not for wealth, lest I forget the
poor. I ask for strength, but not for power, lest I despise
the meek. I ask for wisdom, but not for learning, lest I
scorn the simple. I ask for a clean name, but not for fame,
lest I condemn the lowly. I ask for peace of mind, but not
for idle hours, lest I fail to hearken to the call of duty.*
Inazō Nitobe, 1909; *Quaker faith & practice* 20.01

~

*Silence, to me, allows us to become more aware of how
complex our lives and minds are. Maybe there are different
types of simplicity, one within us and one without us.*
Participant, Friends Southern Senior Conference 2015

~

*You can change and inspire by saying what needs to
be said. You have more power than you know.*
Participant, Friends Summer School 2015

~

*Simplicity isn't just your outside appearance but what
you think on the inside. It's not how other people see you
but how you see yourself and know yourself to be like.*
Participant, Yorkshire Friends Holiday School 2015

~

Young Quakers created the following guidelines for simplicity at Friends Southern Senior Conference 2015. These are simple versions of Richard Foster's ten principles for the expression of simplicity (*Celebration of discipline: the path to spiritual growth*);

* Take the time to realise that our mind's clutter can be just as obstructive as physical and material clutter.

* Appreciate the positive stuff in your life.

* Be generous towards others.

* Question the usefulness and pleasure that you will gain from an item when considering its purchase.

* Take moderately what you need and want, but know your limits.

* Make use of your material possessions.

* Understand the connection between you and the things you consume and where they come from.

* Be independently minded; think critically about the way you consume, and how that is influenced by society.

* Silence can help you develop as a person; embrace it as an alternative to life's constant stimulation.

* Find what simplicity means to you and act upon it.

* Both hoarding and minimalism are too focused on the material – true simplicity is in the mind and is spiritual.

* Simplicity is living adventurously.

Sustainability

Environment | *Equality*

Justice | *Peace*

Responsibility | *Simplicity*

Quakers believe we have a responsibility for protecting the environment and working towards a sustainable world. "The produce of the earth is a gift from our gracious creator to the inhabitants, and to impoverish the earth now to support outward greatness appears to be an injury to the succeeding age" (*Quaker faith & practice* 25.01). These words of John Woolman mean as much to us today as they meant in 1772. This belief is rooted in our testimonies to equality and peace. Sustainability is important to Quakers because we work to see 'that of God' in everyone and in everything.

In Britain many have a comfortable material lifestyle that uses more than our fair share of the world's resources. Quakers regard working against this inequality and seeking justice as a key part in our witness as Quakers. The material greed that can dominate our lives is also challenged by the Quaker testimony to simplicity.

We have long been aware that our behaviour impoverishes the earth, and it is our responsibility both to conserve the earth's resources and to share them more equitably. In 1989, Britain Yearly Meeting minuted that this concern "grows from our faith, and cannot be separated from it. It challenges us to look again at our lifestyles and reassess our priorities, and makes us realise the truth of Ghandi's words: 'Those who say religion has nothing to do with politics do not know what religion is'" (London Yearly Meeting 1989; *Quaker faith & practice* 25.10).

We all need to take responsibility to act on whatever changes we are called to make. At the same time we need to pledge ourselves to act together as communities. "The environmental crisis is enmeshed in global economic injustice and we must face our responsibility, as one of the nations which has unfairly benefited at others' expense, to redress inequalities which, in William Penn's words, are 'wretched and blasphemous'" (Minute 36 of Yearly Meeting, 2011, 'Our Canterbury Commitment').

British Quakers tackle their concern for sustainability on many different levels, thinking nationally about how we as Quakers commit to sustainability and also looking at how we might seek to comment on public policy. Alongside this, we consider how we can campaign and speak out against those things that take us further away from a sustainable society and economy. Local and area Quaker meetings are encouraged to work in their own localities to encourage positive attitudes to sustainability. Individual Quakers are called to consider the effect of their lives on the world's limited resources and in particular on their carbon footprint.

The world is a wonderful resource for our material and spiritual needs. We should treasure it and preserve its capacity to sustain and inspire. That, in turn, calls for a creative responsibility towards the earth we have inherited and for proper sharing of its riches. It means seeing 'that of God' in the world around us and being moved by considerations other than personal gain. Habitats, species and the needs of others are too easily sacrificed to the immediate desires of the present. It cannot be right to leave the world poorer than we found it.

~

Treat the earth well: it was not given to you by your parents;
it was loaned to you by your children.
Kikuyu Proverb

~

All we possess are the gifts of God to us. Now in
distributing it to others, we act as his steward.
John Woolman; *Quaker faith & practice* 20.55

~

Our world is borrowed; some day we must give it
back. We are part of a system, not the controllers.
Participant, Yorkshire Friends Holiday School 2015

~

Everyone has the right to a standard of living adequate for the
health and well-being of himself and his family, including food,
clothing, housing and medical care and necessary social services.
Article 25.1, Universal Declaration of Human Rights, 1948

~

We do not own the world, and its riches are not ours to
dispose of at will. Show a loving consideration for all
creatures and seek to maintain the beauty and variety
of the world. Work to ensure increasing power over
nature is used responsibly, with reverence for life.
Advices & queries 42

~

~

*Four in five of us are, to some extent, members of faith
communities. If just a fraction of this huge body of
believers were to connect their faith to sustainable
development and act accordingly, with the support of
their institutions, the gains could be world-changing.*
Ian Christie, University of Surrey, writing in *Green futures*

~

*Where we see crisis we also see opportunity to remake society as
a communion of people living sustainably as part of the world.*
Meeting for Sufferings, Britain Yearly Meeting, June 2009

~

*You can never have an impact on society
if you have not changed yourself.*
Nelson Mandela (1918–2013)

~

*In a few decades, the relationship between the
environment, resources and conflict may seem
almost as obvious as the connection we see today
between human rights, democracy and peace.*
Wangari Maathai (1940–2011)

~

*There is a duty not only to do no harm
but also to make positive change.*
Participant, Junior Yearly Meeting 2015

~

~

We are here to live with the land, not to take control of the land.
Participant, Britain Yearly Meeting Young People's
Programme 2015

~

*This planet came with a set of instructions, but we seem
to have misplaced them. Important rules like don't poison
the water, soil, or air, don't let the earth get overcrowded,
and don't touch the thermostat have been broken.*
Paul Hawken, 2009

~

Membership

Celebration | *Community*

Convincement | *Discernment*

Meeting | *Truth*

In Britain, around 25,000 people attend Quaker meeting for worship. Around half of these are members of the Religious Society of Friends (Quakers); the others are visitors and people who attend our meetings and are not members (the name we use for them is 'attenders'). Membership links the individual to the community and the organisation. It enables us to have a public voice, to relate to other organisations and to support members and meetings.

Wanting to become a member starts with a Quaker deciding this is something they want to explore. Some people have attended a Quaker meeting for many years without applying for membership. Attenders may be intimately involved in the Society, helping to support the work of the meeting and Quakers more widely, being on rotas, providing financial support and occasionally being involved in committee work and decision making. Some may never seek membership; others, sooner or later, feel moved to do so.

'Convincement' is the word used to describe how people become Quakers. That 'convincement' could be just a slow realisation that this is the right thing to do. Membership is a way of saying that you accept, at least, the fundamental elements of Quakerism. There is no list of what these elements are but it is likely that you know Quakerism well enough to feel you want to be part of a group of like-minded people, part of this community. Perhaps you and the meeting may recognise that you are still searching for the truth, but here and now you are searching along these lines and that, for the present, Quakers are your spiritual home. Membership is never based on 'being worthy' or attaining a certain 'standard of goodness'!

There is a simple procedure for applying to be a member of an area meeting (and therefore of Britain Yearly Meeting). Most often an applicant will have gone through a time of convincement and discernment that this is the right thing for them to do. Each area meeting can develop its own procedures. Often the applicant will write a letter to the area meeting clerk expressing a wish to become a member. Two Quakers will then be appointed (one local and well known to the applicant and one from a different part of the area meeting) to visit the applicant. There will be no set, expected questions or answers, but all three will probably explore and recount stories and ideas about their own spiritual journeys. One of the visiting Quakers will then write a report of the visit, which will be considered and agreed by all three who were at the meeting (including the applicant). This report does not make a recommendation about membership. The report is then considered by the area meeting and a decision is made on membership.

Membership can be seen as an outward expression of what is already there. It is always a cause for quiet celebration! Whether you choose to become a member or remain as an attender, it is important to remember that Quakers have long affirmed the priesthood of all believers. Everyone who is committed to Quakers has a responsibility for the health and maintenance of the meeting community. We are asked to contribute, in whatever ways are most suitable, to the life of the organisation we are part of. We benefit, have fun and hopefully find joy and spiritual fulfilment in working with others.

For online content go to
www.yqspace.org.uk/passages
www.yqspace.org.uk/playlists

~

Friends are together on a pilgrimage of hope. We continue to follow our inward teacher, sometimes falteringly, sometimes confidently, but always in the company of those who have travelled this way before us and those who are journeying with us now.
Epistle from Britain Yearly Meeting 2013

~

I scribbled a one-line letter to the membership clerk as if I had suddenly learnt the art of automatic writing. "Dear Sheila," it said, "I would like to apply for membership of the Religious Society of Friends." Nothing else. I signed it, stamped it and sighed with relief. It wasn't my problem any more. The Quakers could sort it out now. The ways in which they sorted it out I found to be gentle and beguiling.
Geoffrey Durham, *Being a Quaker.*

~

Membership does not require great moral or spiritual achievement, but it does require a sincerity of purpose and a commitment to Quaker values and practices.
Quaker faith & practice 11.01

~

~

For some young people, membership can be a meaningful personal formalisation of their faith. Others felt that Quakerism is defined more by its spirit of community and one's own sense of belonging. It is our shared goals, some of which may be embodied in the Quaker testimonies that bind us together as a religious group.
Minute 1, Junior Yearly Meeting, 2014

~

The Kingdom of Heaven did gather us and catch us all, as in a net, and his heavenly power at one time drew many hundreds to land. We came to know a place to stand in and what to wait in.
Francis Howgill, 1663

~

Decision making

Discernment | Respect

Responsibility | Truth

Upholding | Worship

Quakers make many of their decisions in a Quaker business meeting. This is essentially a meeting for worship, except that it has a pre-arranged agenda; this is why it is known as a 'meeting for worship for business'. Quakers gather in silence and seek the guidance of the Light in the matters before them.

The clerk opens the meeting. Clerks are a cross between a secretary and a chair. They carry a great deal of responsibility for the meeting for business; they will prepare the agenda, undertake the necessary administration and guide the meeting through the business. Often an assistant clerk will sit next to the clerk to help with the tasks and running of the meeting.

Often someone in the meeting will present an item of business and will be asked to answer questions of clarification. Then the meeting will try to discern what is required, in an atmosphere of worship. Spoken contributions are offered as ministry. There will be much use of silence to help consideration of the matter. Silence provides a space to reflect on what people have said, enabling our consideration to move beyond our initial response.

Everyone is welcome and encouraged to be at business meetings. There may be information available beforehand and it is suggested that we come 'with hearts and minds prepared', though open to new leadings. The outcome reflects the feeling of the meeting as a whole. In the meeting it is customary to stand and wait to be called by the clerk if you feel prompted to speak. The point of contributions should be not to win an argument but to uphold the workings of the community. We all strive together to find the way forward, to find what God is calling us to do.

The role of the clerk is to try to discern the outcome of each item, the 'sense of the meeting'. No vote is taken. Eventually a decision will be made that reflects the feeling of the meeting. If Quakers are not comfortable in allowing a decision to be made, the clerk may suggest the business is returned to at a later date, if that is possible. This way of making decisions can be very liberating; it ensures that minority views are not dismissed or ignored. Once a decision is reached the clerk will present a draft minute to the meeting; this will be written while the meeting waits quietly in support of the clerk doing this work.

If a Quaker feels that the draft minute doesn't reflect the sense of the meeting, now is the time to stand, wait to be called and then say so. Amendments may be suggested. It is important to have waited in the Light and eventually reached the right decision. The minute will be re-drafted and read again. The clerk will ask if the minute is acceptable to the meeting, and, if it is, people will respond 'I hope so'. A sensitive clerk will have helped the meeting to find a way forward by encouraging those at the meeting to be silent, to wait and to remember that the group is worshipping together.

Decision making in this way is not an easy process. It takes time, care and love. But it is worth the struggle; when the process works the reward is a powerful sense of rightness and unity. The result can be enlightening, surprising and invigorating.

~

*The unity we seek depends on the willingness of us
all to seek the truth in each other's utterances; on our
being open to persuasion; and in the last resort on a
willingness to recognise and accept the sense of the
meeting as recorded in the minute, knowing that our
dissenting views have been heard and considered.*
Quaker faith & practice 3.06

~

*The job of the participants is to abandon any
preconceived notions and to listen not just to each
other, but crucially to the promptings of love and
truth, to the leadings of God, in their hearts.*
Geoffrey Durham, *Being a Quaker*

~

*Therefore, dear Friends, wait in the Light, that the
word of the Lord may dwell plentifully in you.*
William Dewsbury, 1675; Quaker faith & practice 20.19

~

*Are you prepared to let your insights and personal wishes
take their place alongside those of others or to be set
aside as the meeting seeks the right way forward?*
Advices & queries 15

~

~

We are not to know where we may be led and we may
come to see that our hopes were for things way beyond our
imagination... What is important is being faithful to the next
step and knowing we take it not in our power but in God's.
Ben Pink Dandelion, *Living the Quaker Way*

~

Are your meetings for church affairs held in a spirit of worship
and in dependence on the guidance of God? Remember that
we do not seek a majority decision nor even consensus. As
we wait patiently for divine guidance our experience is that
the right way will open and we shall be led into unity.
Advices & queries 14

~

Listen patiently and seek the truth which other people's opinions
may contain for you. Avoid hurtful criticism and provocative
language. Do not allow the strength of your convictions to
betray you into making statements or allegations that are
unfair or untrue. Think it possible that you may be mistaken.
Advices & queries 17

~

Keep your meetings in the power of God... And when
Friends have finished their business, sit down and wait
quietly and wait upon the Lord to feel him. And go not
beyond the Power, but keep in the Power by which God
almighty may be felt among you... For the power of
the Lord will work through all, if... you follow it.
George Fox, 1658; *Quaker faith & practice* 3.30

~

Life journeys

Community | Death

Education | Friendship

Marriage | Ourselves

Our lives are all a journey, or perhaps a series of journeys. Maybe the journey is more important than the destination. We learn things along the way and become changed by what we experience. Our lives are shaped by things that happen to us. Our journey is influenced and made richer by what we encounter along the way. This in turn shapes and, hopefully, motivates us to make life better for our fellow travellers.

Community

~

The more we listen carefully to one another the closer we come to an intimate connection with the greater whole. We are challenged to become beacons for change in the world and to have the courage to 'hope beyond imagination'.
Epistle of Britain Yearly Meeting 2014

~

~

We cannot seek achievement for ourselves and forget about progress and prosperity for our community... Our ambitions must be broad enough to include the aspirations and needs of others, for their sakes and for our own.
César Chávez, American workers' and civil rights activist
(1927–1993)

~

No man is an island, entire of itself; every man is a piece of the continent, a part of the main. If a clod be washed away by the sea, Europe is the less, as well as if a promontory were, as well as if a manor of thy friend's or of thine own were: any man's death diminishes me, because I am involved in mankind, and therefore never send to know for whom the bells tolls; it tolls for thee.
John Donne (1572–1631)

~

A person is only a person because of other people.
Ubuntu philosophy

~

Our Quaker identity and community supports us when we are in the world and countering its assumptions, and it informs and changes our lives. It helps me in the stands I want to make and it helps me see others I should be making.
Ben Pink Dandelion, *Celebrating the Quaker Way*

~

Death

~

Saturday morning, making chocolate clusters, and you with chocolate all smeared around your rosy mouth, looking very comical, turned to me and said, "Will your body come back again, Grannie, after you are dead?" "No, not this body," I reply, putting a cluster neatly shaped upon the baking tin between us.

"But I'll be around all right, hovering somewhere, laughing with you, feeling quite near as Grandpa does with me." Your thoughts had very nearly moved elsewhere but, satisfied, "That's OK" you said.
Ruth Fawell, 1976; *Quaker faith & practice* 21.53

~

But Death is but crossing the world, as friends do the seas; they live in one another still. For they must needs be present, that love and live in that which is omnipresent. In this divine glass, they see face to face; and their converse is free, as well as pure.
William Penn, 1693

~

Education

~

*Watching a million stars shine, feeling the waves break
on a volcanic beach, being moved by reading the next
line, being shocked by painting that colour... discovering
that living adventurously can free the spirit. We all
need to experience education, not just receive it.*
Graham Ralph, *Faith and Practice at a Quaker School.*

~

*Educating the mind without educating
the heart is no education at all.*
Aristotle (384–322BC)

~

Friendship

~

*Do you cherish your friendships, so that they grow in
depth and understanding and mutual respect? In close
relationships we may risk pain as well as finding joy.
When experiencing great happiness or great hurt we
may be more open to the working of the spirit.*
Advices & queries 21

~

~

That best portion of a good man's life,
His little, nameless, unremembered acts
Of kindness and of love.
William Wordsworth, 'Tintern Abbey'

~

Marriage

~

Friends, I take this my friend _____ to be my spouse,
promising, through God's help, to be unto him/her a loving
and faithful spouse, so long as we both on earth shall live.
Quaker faith & practice 16.42

~

Quaker marriage is not an alternative form of marriage
available to the general public, but is for members and
those who, whilst not being in formal membership,
are in unity with its religious nature and witness.
Quaker faith & practice 16.04

~

For the right joining in marriage is the work of the Lord
only, and not the priests' or the magistrates'; for it is God's
ordinance and not man's; and therefore Friends cannot
consent that they should join them together: for we marry
none; it is the Lord's work, and we are but witnesses.
George Fox, 1669; Quaker faith & practice 16.01

~

Ourselves

~

*Through our discussions we recognised our anxieties and
fears. We realised that we are individuals and that we are
alone but, as part of a loving community, to be alone does
not necessarily mean to be lonely. We discovered that it is
acceptable to have confused feelings, to be different, to do
things our own way. We should not feel guilty when we are
wrong, and appreciate that there must be room for mistakes.
There are people who want us to be exactly as we are.*
Epistle of Junior Yearly Meeting 1991

~

*We work for a more just and peaceful world, one with less
discrimination and greater equality, a more sustainable
approach to the economy and to the planet, and a greater
degree of integrity amongst those entrusted with power
and responsibility. We feel these certainties deeply, beyond
conscious choice. These values are who we are. They affect
what we buy and where we shop, how or if we travel, how
we are in the workplace. We try not to be dissuaded from
doing the right thing just because it is unpopular. We
are active in all kinds of organisations to try to achieve
these ends, not in our own power, but based on the holy
imperatives given us in worship. We care passionately.*
Ben Pink Dandelion, *Living the Quaker Way*

~

~

*True Godliness don't turn men out of the world, but
enables them to live better in it, and excites their
endeavours to mend it: not to hide their candle under
a bushel, but set it upon a table in a candlestick.*
William Penn, 1682; Quaker faith & practice 23.02

~

*Our deepest fear is not that we are inadequate. Our deepest fear
is that we are powerful beyond measure. It is our light, not our
darkness that most frightens us. We ask ourselves, Who am I to
be brilliant, gorgeous, talented, fabulous? Actually, who are you
not to be? You are a child of God. Your playing small does not
serve the world. There is nothing enlightened about shrinking
so that other people won't feel insecure around you. We are all
meant to shine, as children do. We were born to make manifest
the glory of God that is within us. It's not just in some of us; it's
in everyone, and as we let our own light shine, we unconsciously
give other people permission to do the same. As we are liberated
from our own fear, our presence automatically liberates others.*
Marianne Williamson, *A Return to Love: Reflections on the
Principles of A Course in Miracles*

~

For online content go to
www.yqspace.org.uk/passages
www.yqspace.org.uk/playlists

Advices and queries as compiled by young Quakers

The 42 *Advices & queries* of the Religious Society of Friends are a series of reflections and promptings that are reminders of the insights of the Society. Quakers use the *Advices & queries* as a source of challenge and inspiration in their personal lives and in their life as a community.

Young Quakers created the advices and queries given below at Junior Yearly Meeting in 2015. They are simple versions of each of the full advices and queries. They aim to be accessible while still containing insights into how to live faithfully.

1. Be true to yourself.

2. Try to be spiritual in all aspects of life.

3. Enjoy silence.

4. Remember our Christian heritage.

5. Use religious literature if it's helpful.

6. Multifaith communities are a source of richness.

7. Notice unexpected moments of spirituality in all parts of your life.

8. Value worship, by yourself or with others.

9. Consider your whole self – good and bad – in worship.

10. Come to meeting regardless of your mood; it'll make you feel better.

11. Be honest with yourself.

12. Try to stay focused in meeting.

13. When you feel moved to speak, speak.

14. You're not always right; listen to others.

15. Take some responsibility in your meeting.

16. Be open to different ways of doing Quakerism.

17. Everyone thinks of God differently; don't be judgemental.

18. Be welcoming to everyone. We've all got stuff going on, don't judge a book by its cover.

19. Children and young people are great; look after them and learn from them.

20. Talk about your beliefs and put them into action.

21. Enjoy time with friends, but also take time to challenge each other.

22. Don't be disrespectful or judgemental. Embrace diversity.

23. Marriage isn't just a legal contract, it's a religious pairing.

24. Sometimes it's difficult to work with children, but it's worth it.

25. Relationships take time and effort. Talk!

26. Appreciate your family.

27. Live adventurously.

28. Life is full of learning. Change always happens.

29. Don't worry about getting old.

30. We all die; accept it and support each other.

31. War is bad. No long-term good ever comes from it.

32. Be aware of prejudices and try to work past them.

33. Try to understand the causes of injustice and change them.

34. Don't just live in your own little bubble; there's a big world out there.

35. Sometimes breaking the law is necessary. But think about it and get some advice first.

36. People worry about different things – help them make positive change even if it's not your worry.

37. Be honest, truthful and open.

38. Don't give in to peer pressure.

39. Question the pressures of mainstream culture.

40. Be careful with drugs and alcohol.

41. Try to live simply.

42. Look after the world for the future. Reduce, reuse and recycle.

Organisation of Quakerism

Meeting for worship

Central to the practice and organisation of Quakers is the meeting for worship. As well as being our way of worship, it underpins how we make decisions in meeting for worship for business at every level of the Society. For more information see chapters 'Meeting for worship' and 'Decision making' (pp. 11 and 65).

Quaker structures

The following explanations draw on 'Quakers in Britain: A short guide to our structures' (Quakers in Britain 2014).

The individual Quaker

Because Quaker meetings for worship are open to everyone, the body of worshippers in Quakerism is made up of those who are members of the Society and those who are not members but regularly attend a particular local meeting ('attenders'). An attender can become a member through a simple process (see the chapter on 'Membership', p. XX). Most local meetings have both attenders and members.

Local meeting

The local meeting is made up of Quakers who worship together. In addition to being responsible for holding weekly meetings for worship, the local meeting will have business meetings to deal with local matters. There is also a responsibility to nurture the spiritual life of the meeting and to ensure pastoral care of the members and attenders. Local meetings prepare for area business meetings and send representatives to them as well as reporting as appropriate.

Area meeting

An area meeting is a group of local meetings. When you become a member, your membership is with your area meeting, not your local meeting or Britain Yearly Meeting. The area meeting is the main body for 'church' affairs. Its role is to develop and maintain a community of Quakers, a family of local meetings who gather for worship and spiritual enrichment. The area meeting is also the body that has legal responsibility for property (e.g. meeting houses), employment matters (e.g. meeting house wardens), pastoral care, membership and marriage arrangements, and recording the deaths of members in the area. Area meetings hold regular business meetings.

National bodies

In addition to area meetings, Scotland and Wales have national bodies with particular responsibilities for Quakers in those countries. These are the General Meeting for Scotland and the Meeting of Friends in Wales (Cyfarfod y Cyfeillion yng Nghymru).

Meeting for Sufferings

Meeting for Sufferings is the standing representative body entrusted with the general care of matters affecting Britain Yearly Meeting. In the intervals between yearly meetings, it makes decisions and issues statements in the name of Britain Yearly Meeting. Meeting for Sufferings was originally set up to establish and record the persecution of Quakers and to seek help on their behalf. Today Meeting for Sufferings is concerned with major policy decisions. It is made up of representatives from each area meeting.

The Young People's Participation Day is an annual national event that happens at the same time and in the same place as Meeting for Sufferings. It is an opportunity for young Quakers to be involved in decisions that affect them and the organisation they are a part of. The day offers the chance for participants to consider items on the Meeting for Sufferings agenda that are of relevance to young people, and to identify issues that might be of relevance to Meeting for Sufferings.

Britain Yearly Meeting: The gathering

In England, Scotland, Wales, the Channel Islands and the Isle of Man, Britain Yearly Meeting is the body to which all Quakers belong. It is also the name of the annual gathering, often referred to simply as 'Yearly Meeting', in which Quakers from all over Britain come together for worship, business, support, sharing of concerns and friendship. Yearly Meeting has programmes for children and young people, including Junior Yearly Meeting and the Young People's Programme.

Junior Yearly Meeting (JYM) is an event for young Quakers in Britain. Participants represent area meetings, Quaker schools or overseas yearly meetings and other religious groups; 'open' places are also available, for which any young Quaker can apply. As a youth event JYM is planned and facilitated by its own arrangements committee (with the support of adults). The committee is a group of young people appointed by their peers who agree the theme and create a programme for the event, which links to issues being considered at Britain Yearly Meeting (BYM). As well as writing an 'epistle', JYM may write a minute reflecting discernment on the issues considered by BYM. The clerks of JYM will read the JYM epistle in Yearly Meeting.

The *BYM Young People's Programme* is a national residential event that happens at the same time as BYM and is planned by young people (appointed by their peers at the previous year's event) with the support of adults. The Young People's Programme is a chance to engage with the themes of Yearly Meeting through a variety of creative activities. It provides an opportunity to consider our Quaker faith and think about how we live as Quakers in the world today. As with the JYM epistle, at the end of Yearly Meeting the minute of the Young People's Programme, which is written by and agreed by the participants of the event, is received by the adult Yearly Meeting.

Britain Yearly Meeting: The organisation

Britain Yearly Meeting of the Religious Society of Friends (Quakers) is the national body of British Quakers. It is a registered charity and has trustees, appointed by Yearly Meeting. Much of the centrally managed work is based at Friends House in London. The organisation employs about 150 staff who undertake work on behalf of the Yearly Meeting. The staff are overseen by Yearly Meeting Trustees. They work within five departments, reporting to the Recording Clerk, who is the senior member of staff.

The four major committees for centrally managed work are: Quaker Life Central Committee, Quaker Peace and Social Witness Central Committee, Quaker Committee for Christian and Interfaith Relations and Quaker World Relations Committee.

Roles in Quakerism

Nominations committees

A nominations committee is an appointed group of Quakers entrusted with trying to find people willing and able to serve a meeting in various ways (e.g. to be clerks, elders, overseers). Having discerned as best they can the gifts and talents of those available, they 'bring their names' or 'nominate' them to the meeting concerned. For details on some of the various roles, see below.

Clerk

The Quaker responsible for the conduct of a meeting for business. The clerk will try to discern the 'sense of the meeting' (see below under 'Quaker terms') and help Quakers agree written minutes of any decisions. Clerks are usually appointed for a three-year term of service.

Elders

A Group of Quakers who have a particular responsibility for the spiritual life of the local meeting. They will make sure that meetings for worship are rightly held (they will shake hands to end the meeting), they may arrange study groups and they will organise funerals and memorial meetings. Elders are usually appointed for a three-year term of service.

Overseers

Group of Quakers from a local meeting who have a particular responsibility for the pastoral care of the members and attenders of the meeting. They advise individuals on applications for membership and befriend in order to help when personal difficulties arise. Overseers are usually appointed for a three-year term of service.

Registering officer

Each area meeting appoints a suitable Quaker as registering officer. The officer's role is to oversee marriage procedures and to register all marriages solemnised according to the custom of the Society within that area meeting.

Recording Clerk

The senior member of staff, who leads the Britain Yearly Meeting staff team. The Recording Clerk is appointed by Britain Yearly Meeting Trustees, is responsible for interpreting Quaker church government and acts as secretary to various Quaker bodies including Yearly Meeting, Meeting for Sufferings and Britain Yearly Meeting Trustees.

Words used by Quakers

Advices & queries
A reminder to Quakers of the insights of the Society. This series of 42 reflections and promptings is used by Quakers for challenge and inspiration in our personal lives and our lives in the world. (See the chapter 'Advices and queries as compiled by young Quakers', p. 79).

Clearness
The state of having reached clarity about the way forward, after searching for a response to a concern or dilemma. This is often achieved by having a 'meeting for clearness'.

Concern
A deep leading from the spirit prompting action on a particular matter that is subject to testing within the Quaker community.

Conflict resolution
Also known as reconciliation, conflict resolution is the process of facilitating the finding of a peaceful solution to a disagreement among two or more parties.

Convincement
As in 'Quaker by convincement': one who has become convinced of the truth of the Quaker way.

Discernment
The process by which Quakers try to sense what is truly from God.

Friend
A term used within Quakerism for a member of the Religious Society of Friends. It can be used interchangeably with 'Quaker' (a name that more people are familiar with).

Friends Ambulance Unit
An organisation set up in World War I that enabled Quakers (and other conscientious objectors) to serve the injured in war zones without bearing arms.

Gathered
The term used by Quakers to describe a meeting for worship where there is a tangible sense of togetherness with one another and with that something outside ourselves that we may call God.

'I hope so'
Positive response to a question of Quaker business. For example, after the clerk of a meeting reads out a drafted minute of a decision, he or she will ask, 'Is this minute acceptable to Friends?' If it is, Quakers will usually respond, 'I hope so.' This is because each Quaker can only answer for his or her own discernment, not anyone else's, and hopes to have correctly discerned the will of God.

Light
The presence of God in our hearts and lives, which shows us the truth and gives us strength to act. 'Truth' is often used in a similar way.

Ministry
Often this term refers to spoken ministry, which means standing in a meeting for worship and expressing out loud the leadings of the Spirit. You may have little firm idea of what words are going to come out but suddenly, sometimes shaking, you will find yourself on your feet talking. However, 'ministry' also has the broader sense of everything

we give to others – how we 'minister' to them – as we live out our lives.

Minute

The record of a business meeting decision, capturing the 'sense of the meeting' (see below). The minute is written in the meeting and read aloud by the clerk, and is agreed – sometimes after alteration – by the assembled members.

Quaker faith & practice

An anthology of Quakers' testimonies, beliefs, reflections and practices. The book provides spiritual guidance and also details the structure and procedures of the Religious Society of Friends (Quakers). This is where all the information on procedures for membership, marriage, business, the structure of the Society and the spiritual experience that underpins them will be found.

Religious Society of Friends

The formal name for Quakers. Quakers use the term 'Religious Society of Friends' to reflect that they are a faith community with worship at its heart.

Sense of the meeting

In reaching decisions in business meetings, Quakers do not vote. After full consideration of a matter and allowing for new insights to develop, the collective decision of the Meeting is gathered and expressed by the clerk, in a minute, for the approval of the meeting. This is not a consensus; individuals are asked to accept the sense of the meeting, which may not be their own personal view.

Testimonies

Convictions based on the experience of Quakers that have given direction to their lives. They attempt to put faith into practice. The testimonies do not exist in any rigid, written form, nor are they imposed. All Quakers have to search for the ways in which testimonies can become true for them. There are testimonies for truth and integrity, equality, peace and simplicity and a developing testimony around sustainability.

That of God in everyone
This is the core Quaker belief that the divine can be experienced in everyone. This is reflected in the following expression by George Fox "... walk cheerfully [courageously] over the world, answering that of God in every one."

Unprogrammed meeting
The style of meeting for worship in use in Britain and Europe, following the tradition established by George Fox and the early Quakers. These meetings are held in silence and ministry springs from that silence; they do not use a pre-determined programme.

Upholding *or* holding in the light
To silently hold in one's thoughts and heart someone who is experiencing joy or sorrow, or who is making a decision. Upholding may also be used in the context of a business meeting, for example upholding the clerk during the writing of a minute.

Some dates in Quaker history

1647	George Fox recognises God's light is within everyone
1652	Birth of Quakerism in the north of England
1655	Margaret Fell shapes national Quaker organisation
1660	Restoration of the monarchy – systematic persecution of Quakers
1661	Quakers present their peace testimony to Charles II
1681	William Penn establishes the Quaker state of Pennsylvania
1689	Act of Toleration allows Quakers to worship legally
1755	Quaker marriage becomes legal
1758	Quakers begin campaigning to abolish slavery
1796	Quakers pioneer humane mental care at The Retreat, York
1813	Elizabeth Fry starts her prison reform work at Newgate Prison
1825	Quaker firms open first steam railway, 'Stockton & Darlington'
1870s	Growth of Quaker chocolate makers Cadbury and Rowntree

1890s	Fair-trading Quaker banks Barclays and Lloyds thrive
1920	First conference of Quakers worldwide
1927	Friends House opens as the home of Quakers in Britain
1938	Quakers evacuate children from Nazi Germany on the Kindertransport
1947	Quakers awarded Nobel Peace Prize for their war relief work
1997	Quakers work at the United Nations to bring about the Mine Ban Treaty
2009	Quakers in Britain campaign for same-sex marriage
2014	Quakers in Britain disinvest from fossil fuels

Links, events and more information

A website for young Quakers:
www.yqspace.org.uk

Information about events for young Quakers:
www.yqspace.org.uk/events

Links to supportive organisations offering advice,
information or support:
www.yqspace.org.uk/advice

Links to the Children and Young People team at Friends
House, and to a selection of Quaker and non-Quaker
organisations:
www.yqspace.org.uk/contacts

Faith and Practice at a Quaker school:
www.aquakereducation.co.uk/home/pdf_download

Britain Yearly Meeting (the organisation):
Friends House, 173 Euston Road, London NW1 2BJ
(tel. 020 7663 1000).
www.quaker.org.uk

Quaker faith & practice online:
http://qfp.quaker.org.uk/

Information about Quaker work for peace and justice:
www.quaker.org.uk/working-peace

'Be the change', a resource to help young Quakers to take action on issues of Quaker concern: www.yqspace.org.uk/bethechange

Events

Summer events for young Quakers

Residential weeks of new experiences, spiritual growth, friendship and fun. For information go to www.yqspace.org.uk/find-event.

The Friends Summer School
Ages 11 to 17 from northwest and central England, mid-Wales and Borders, north Wales and Derbyshire, but young people from other areas are also welcome.

FSSE Junior Gathering
Ages 11 to 14 from the south of England and Wales. www.fsse.org.uk

Friends Southern Senior Conference
Ages 15 to 18 from the south of England and Wales. www.fsse.org.uk

Northern Young Friends Summer Shindig
Ages 11 to 16 from Scotland, Northumbria, Cumbria, the rest of the UK and beyond!

Yorkshire Friends Holiday School
Ages 13 to 18 from Yorkshire (open to applications from elsewhere).
www.yfhs.org.uk

Link groups and area meeting events for young Quakers

Day events, social gatherings and residential weekends for young Quakers to come together from across an area to have fun, build friendships and explore Quakerism. For information go to www.yqspace.org.uk/find-event.

More information

Young Friends General Meeting is the national organisation for young adult Quakers aged 18–30.
www.yfgm.quaker.org.uk

Quaker chaplains work in a wide variety of colleges and universities around the country. They offer pastoral support and provide a visible Quaker presence within an organisation. They also serve as a point of contact and support for young Quakers going away to college or university. They are available to students who have just heard about Quakerism and would like to know more.
www.quaker.org.uk/university-chaplains

The Woodbrooke Quaker Study Centre offers many opportunities for young adult Quakers aged 18–30, running a number of courses specifically for young Friends and a Young Adult Leadership Programme as a part of their education programme.
www.woodbrooke.org.uk/pages/young-adults.html

Quaker organisations

The Leaveners is a Quaker performing-arts project. Its members run workshops for meetings and residential theatre, music, singing and creative arts events.
www.leaveners.org
www.facebook.com/Leaveners

Quaker Action on Alcohol and Drugs (QAAD) works to meet the need for support and information in relation to alcohol, other drugs and gambling.
www.qaad.org

QAAD occasionally runs events for young people and has produced a DVD, 'Too much too young', exploring the health and social effects of alcohol on young people today.
www.qaad.org

Other resources

Resources for working with young people:
www.quaker.org.uk/working-with-12-to-18-years

Cafod Youth Topics: monthly activities on world issues.
www.cafod.org.uk/education

Christian Aid: resource for young people.
http://learn.christianaid.org.uk/

The British Youth Council is a youth-led charity that represents the views of young people to the government, decision makers and the media.
www.byc.org.uk

Bibliography

Carter, Sydney Bertram (1964). *There's a light that is shining* (George Fox). London: Stainer & Bell Ltd.

Christie, Ian (2011). 'Faith: The largest source of social capital'. Accessed online at www.forumforthefuture.org/greenfutures/articles/faith-largest-source-social-capital. London: Forum for the Future.

Durham, Geoffrey (2011). *Being a Quaker: A guide for newcomers.* London: Quaker Quest.

Foster, Richard (with Kathryn A. Helmers) (2008). *Celebration of discipline: The path to spiritual growth* (Study Guide Edition). London: Hodder & Stoughton.

Friends School of Baltimore (2003). *Faith and Practice.* Baltimore: Friends School of Baltimore.

Hawken, Paul (2009). Commencement Address to the Class of 2009, University of Portland, 3 May. Accessed online at www.up.edu/commencement/default.aspx?cid=9456.

Henrysson, Elin (2012). Journal letter of the Britain Yearly Meeting peaceworker scheme.

Maraboli, Steve (2013). *Unapologetically You: Reflections on Life and the Human Experience.* Logan, Utah: A Better Today Publishing.

Mitchell, David (1999). *Ghostwritten.* London: Hodder & Stoughton.

Penn, William (2001). *Fruits of Solitude* Vol. I, Part 3. The Harvard Classics. New York: P.F. Collier & Son.

Pink Dandelion, Ben (2010). *Celebrating the Quaker way.* London: Quaker Books.

Quaker faith & practice: The book of Christian discipline of the Yearly Meeting of the Religious Society of Friends (Quakers) in Britain (5th ed., 2013). London: Britain Yearly Meeting.

Ralph, Graham (2013). *Faith and Practice at a Quaker School.* York: Quacks Books.

Smith, Robert Lawrence (1999). *A Quaker book of wisdom. Life lessons in simplicity, service, and common sense.* New York: HarperCollins.

Tagore, Rabindranath (2007). *The English Writings of Rabindranath Tagore (volume two: poems).* New Delhi: Atlantic Publishers and Distributors.

Williamson, Marianne (1992). *A Return to Love: Reflections on the Principles of A Course in Miracles.* New York: HarperCollins.